T0017812

MY FIRST Kitten

By Alyssa Satin Capucilli

Photographs by Jill Wachter

Ready-to-Read

Simon Spotlight
New York   London   Toronto   Sydney   New Delhi

SIMON SPOTLIGHT
An imprint of Simon & Schuster Children's Publishing Division
1230 Avenue of the Americas, New York, New York 10020
This Simon Spotlight edition December 2020
Text copyright © 2020 by Alyssa Satin Capucilli
Photographs and illustrations © 2020 by Simon & Schuster, Inc.
For information about special discounts for bulk purchases, please contact
Simon & Schuster Special Sales at 1-866-506-1949 or business@simonandschuster.com.
Manufactured in the United States of America 1020 LAK
2 4 6 8 10 9 7 5 3 1
This book has been cataloged by the Library of Congress.
ISBN 978-1-5344-7754-4 (hc)
ISBN 978-1-5344-7753-7 (pbk)
ISBN 978-1-5344-7755-1 (eBook)

Something soft and furry
is coming home with me.

It is my new kitten.

She is as sweet as can be!

I give my kitten food
and fresh water, too.

My kitten sees the litter box.

He knows just what to do.

My kitten likes to pounce
and play.

My kitten likes to run.

Kittens love to climb up high.

A scratching post is fun!

Kittens like to explore.

I put my things away.

I can keep her safe

each and every day.

My kitten sniffs my hand.

I softly pet his fur.

I use a gentle voice.

I can hear her purr!

Naptime! Naptime!

Kittens need to sleep.

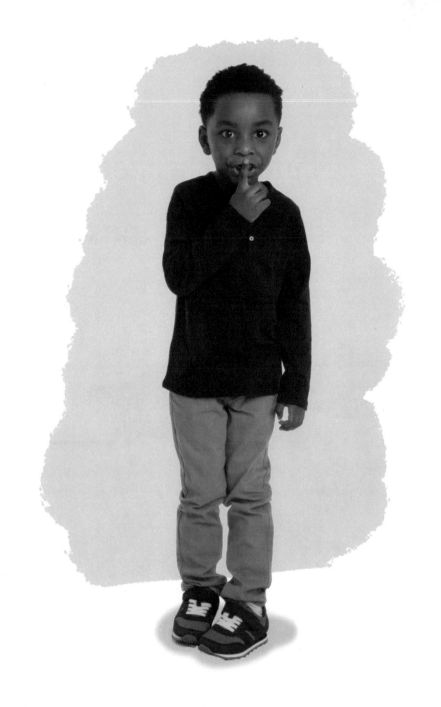

She curls up in her bed.

I do not make a peep!

Time for a checkup,
from tail to toes!

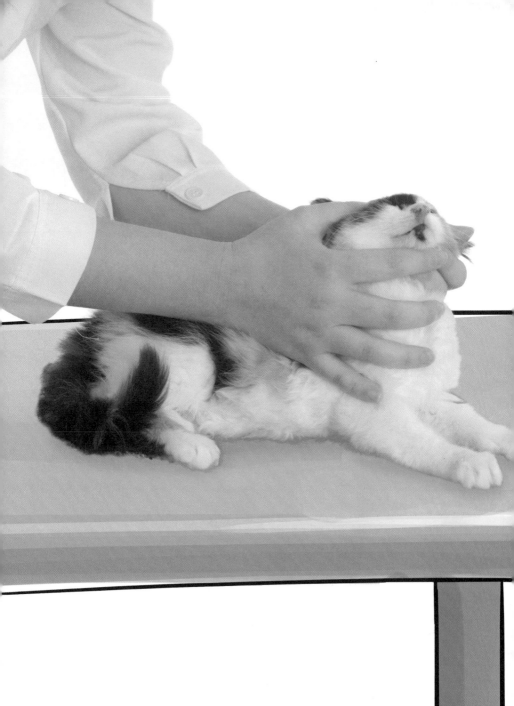

We check my kitten's ears
and her soft pink nose!

My kitten grows each day
with food, play, and rest.

I love my fuzzy friend.

New kittens are the best!

Your New Pet!

Are you ready to care for a new pet?

Let's learn about what a new kitten needs!

Ask a grown-up to help you care for

your special friend.

Welcome Home!

1 Cozy bed

Is your kitten striped? Does it have orange fur?
Gray or black fur? No matter which kitten you've chosen,
all kittens need a clean, quiet,
and comfortable place to sleep.
You can use a cardboard box lined
with a blanket or a soft bed.

2 Litter box

You can introduce your kitten to a litter box right away.

A grown-up can gently rub a kitten's paws in the litter.

The kitten will know what to do!

Always be sure to wash your hands after you are near the litter box.

It's important to set up your kitten's food and water dishes in an area away from the litter box.

Getting to Know You!

1 Sniffing

Kittens are curious! They can use their sense of smell and touch to get to know you. Keep your palm up so your kitten can easily sniff your hand. Let your kitten explore his or her new home slowly and at his or her own pace.

2 Purring and More

ROAR! Did you know kittens are part of the same family as lions, tigers, and other big cats? They may not roar like a lion, but they can let us know how they are feeling.

A soft purr can mean your kitten is happy!

A meow may mean your kitten needs some attention.

A hiss or a rounded back may mean your kitten is frightened or unhappy. Use a calm voice and let your kitten relax before you approach him or her.

Meow!

Playtime!

1 Toys

Kittens love to play! A paper bag is fun for a kitten to pounce on. Kittens also love to chase balls and small stuffed animals. Be careful not to give your kitten anything with sharp edges.

2 Tricks

Did you know that you can teach your kitten a trick?
Some kittens like to jump through hoops.
You can reward your kitten with a healthy treat, like catnip.

3 Climbing

Kittens are natural climbers. A scratching post that's not too high is best for plenty of exercise. It also helps to keep their claws from getting too sharp.

A Healthy Pet!

1 Food, Water, and More

Fresh food, clean water, and exercise will help your kitten grow strong.

2 Cleanup

You can help keep your kitten safe. Always clean up any small things your kitten might nibble on, so he or she doesn't swallow them by mistake. Be sure there are no long wires or cords for a kitten to get tangled in.

3 Checkups

A checkup with the veterinarian will make sure your kitten is healthy. The vet will even look at your kitten's whiskers! Whiskers can help kittens sense objects and the space around them . . . even in the dark!

Your Furry Friend!

With lots of love and care, your new kitten will soon grow into a cat.

It's fun to spend time talking, playing, and interacting with your kitten every day.

Remember that kittens and cats need plenty of quiet time to nap too.

When you hear your kitten's gentle purr, you'll know you've made a new best friend!

Whether you choose a kitten, a cat, or any other pet, you're sure to have fun. You're sure to learn a lot too!

Is your family thinking of getting a new pet?
Consider adopting a pet from a local animal shelter.
Many pets need homes and a best friend like you!